Ice Cream Dream

Written by Jeanne Willis

Illustrated by Jane Cope

Harcourt Supplemental Publishers

Rigby • Steck-Vaughn

www.steck-vaughn.com

One little lemming
Had a lovely dream
All about a sailor man
Serving free ice cream.

He called his little sister
And got her out of bed.
"Free ice cream! Free ice cream!
Follow me!" he said.

Two little lemmings
Were sitting on a bus.
"Free ice cream!" they called.
"Come and follow us!"

"It's very, very tasty.
  Come with us and see.
  Get your lovely ice cream—
  Lovely food for free!"

Three little lemmings
Went running down the street.
"Free ice cream!" they called—
"As much as you can eat!"

"It's very, very tasty.
  Come with us and see.
  Get your lovely ice cream—
  Lovely food for free!"

Four little lemmings
Were sitting on a train.
They were going to the bay
In the wind and rain.

"Free ice cream!" they called.
"Come with us and see.
   Get your lovely ice cream—
   Lovely food for free!"

Five little lemmings
All got to their feet.
"Free ice cream!" they called—
"As much as you can eat!"

"We know where to get it!
Come with us and see.
Grab your lovely ice cream—
Lovely food for free!"

Six little lemmings
Went riding in a van.
"Get your ice cream!" they called—
"Get it from the sailor man!
It's very, very tasty,
And it's free today.
Get your lovely ice cream!
Come to Sailor's Bay!"

Seven little lemmings
Went riding in a truck.
"We want ice cream," they called,
"And today we're in luck.
It's very, very tasty.
Come with us and see.
Get your lovely ice cream—
Lovely food for free!"

Eight little lemmings
Went running up a hill.
"Free ice cream!" they called.
"Isn't that a thrill?
We know where to get it.
Come with us and see.
Grab your lovely ice cream—
Lovely food for free!"

Nine little lemmings
Went running up a cliff—
Nine little lemmings
Going sniff, sniff, sniff!
"We can smell the ice cream
From the sailor man.
Smell the lovely ice cream!
Let's eat it while we can!"

Ten little lemmings
Went running off the top.
They fell into the sea—
Plop, plop, plop!
And what about the sailor man
And the ice cream that was free?
The lemmings forgot all about them.
It was such fun in the sea!